Katerina Brac

CHRISTOPHER REID

Katerina Brac

faber and faber

LONDON · BOSTON

First published in 1985
by Faber and Faber Limited
3 Queen Square London WC1N 3AU

Phototypeset by Wilmaset Birkenhead Merseyside
Printed in Great Britain by
Redwood Burn Ltd Trowbridge Wiltshire

British Library Cataloguing in Publication Data

Reid, Christopher
Katerina Brac
I. Title
821'.914   PR6068.E426

ISBN 0–571–13700–8
ISBN 0–571–13614–1 Pbk

To Het and Bertie

Grateful acknowledgement is hereby made to the editors of the *Poetry Book Society Supplement*, *Poetry Review* and of *The Honest Ulsterman*, where some of these poems have appeared; and also to the editor of *Grand Street* who has published the following poems in his magazine: 'A Tune', 'When the Bullfrogs are in Love', 'History and Parody', 'On the Subject of Fingers and Thumbs', 'Eyebrows Almost Spoke', 'The South', 'What the Uneducated Old Woman Told Me' and 'Screens'. The author is indebted to the Arts Council of Great Britain for the award of a Writer's Bursary.

Contents

Pale-Blue Butterflies

Once again, magically
and without official notification,
it was the time of the year
for the pale-blue butterflies to arrive.

They came in their millions –
an army composed entirely of stragglers
filling the sky,
the gust-driven trash of migration.

Working in the garden,
bent on our solicitous pillage
of the strawberry beds,
out of the corners of our eyes
we saw the first of them descend.

What were we to these multitudinous creatures?
A point of reference
on the transcontinental journey
from A to B?
Hardly even that.

For a week they came
lighting on our favoured blooms,
as detachable as earrings,
but so common
that nobody, except the wobbliest of toddlers,
bothered to try to catch them.

Yet it was not exactly
a mutual indifference.
I'm sure that I was not alone
in feeling, as I do each year,
that this would be the perfect time
to mend the whole of one's life.

Later, when the butterflies had gone,
we loaded our van with the last of the
                                    strawberries
and drove to town
to be given the official market price.

There followed an unscheduled
season of summer thunders:
colossal rearrangements
somewhere at the back of the mind.

A Tune

Stammered on a mandolin,
an old sentimental tune
from an open doorway in summer:
of course, it's only a radio thinking aloud
and nobody paying much attention.
Who can afford to lose tears over music these days?

I have heard the same song
in numerous clever disguises –
embellished with hesitations and surprise chords
by my cousin, the promising fiddler;
crooned almost silently by women in kitchens
to lull children or coax the rising of the dough.

And then there was the dance band
that came twice a year to our village.
My father explained the workings of the bass tuba,
how the breath was obliged to travel patiently
through those shiny intestines, before it could issue
in a sound halfway between serious and rude.

Its thoughtful flatulence underscored
both the quick dances, and the slow ones
where the men took the women in their proprietorial
                                        embrace
and moved about the floor with an ostentatious
                                        dreaminess.
The band played an arrangement of the very tune
that someone's radio is remembering right now.

I dare say it means something to you as well.
Amazing, how a piece of nonsense like this can survive,
more obstinate than any national anthem.
Perhaps they will dig it out again for my funeral:
a six-piece band ought to be sufficient,
with wind, an accordion, drums and at least one
                                        ceremonious tuba.

Son of Memory

So the Muse of History is a man!
I ought to have known long ago.
The clues seem obvious now:
those big black ministerial clodhoppers
jutting from beneath the Attic drapery,
the rasp of that sisterly kiss.

It turns out that he has never been comfortable
in the uniform of the Daughters of Memory,
preferring, when it comes to business,
the manly clank of a suit of armour
or the no-nonsense Esperanto of khaki –
understood these days all over the world.

You may have had dealings with him yourself:
the functionary in the dark office
scanning your documents for a slip of the pen,
or the raincoated fellow who, if you catch his eye,
pretends to be utterly engrossed
in a window full of identical boxes.

Plainly, one can't be too careful.
It's hard to trust a living soul
when even mythology is suspect.
I'm beginning to have my doubts
about Terpsichore's clumping gait
and Erato's fondness for barrackroom metres.

When the Bullfrogs are in Love

On those nights when the bullfrogs are in love
and their ratchety bass thrum keeps me from sleeping,
I have time to chart my position on the map of the sky.

Under night's aegis we rejoin the universe.
The moon, the stars, the mating frogs and I
are linked in a dizzy rapprochement across the
                                        light-years.

I like things to be accurate, and generally
you are included too, although you are probably fast
                                        asleep
in your room in the city from which the stars are
                                        invisible.

Long ago I would have been happily lying beside you,
for all the city's conspiratorial mutter
and the stairwell that waited beyond your apartment door

like the deepest, most superhumanly patient of ears.
In the end, of course, we were separated.
Now I am back in the country, out of harm's way,

I write poems and make the best of what I have.
Unable to ignore the frogs and their gutsy amours,
I let them spin with me among the constellations.

Epithalamium

An intimacy
like the brisk to-and-fro
of small coins,
your fingers thinking.

Something as homely
as a cat or a clock.
But what you leave unsaid
sustains you
like the net of the heavens.

Man and wife
with your life between you
like a chessboard:
a palimpsest
of innumerable possibilities.

Annals

Someone ought to write
the annals of the villages
on this bank of the river.
Conferences, statutes
and the economic forecasts
printed in the newspaper
are naturally important,
but there is much to learn, too,
from the sayings of old women
and the deaths of pigs.
I wish to propose
that a trustworthy historian
chosen by the Ministry of Culture
should spend some time among us.
He would meet my neighbour, the patriarch,
ninety years old,
who lies all day in bed
under a patchwork coverlet
which is really a symbolic map of Heaven,
but knows where every cucumber grows
and how much it will fetch
at the market in town.
His oldest son is a specialist
in the science of clouds
and never gets the weather wrong.
Of his seven children,
five of them female,
there is none without some deep knowledge:
of the different kinds of *eau de vie*,
of the magic language of cursing,
of money, flowers, childbed.
Beyond them lives the village mechanic,

a pious and reclusive man.
He attends all celebrations, however,
where music is required,
playing his violin faster and faster,
before wrapping it up again
in a square of black velvet
and returning home with it alone.
A boy in the village
is learning the Bible off by heart;
there are bets on when he will reach
the end of Deuteronomy.
The priest drinks too much,
but will give anyone who asks for it
his recipe against mosquito bites.
Last year two notable deaths occurred:
one woman was lifted by the wind
and deposited in the river,
where malevolent spirits dragged her to the bottom;
another choked, it is said,
on a fragment of fingernail.
Our landscape is enriched
by rumour and the discussion of prodigies.
Every day, history takes place,
even when nothing happens.
I believe these things should be written down
and published in the metropolis
as a matter of national pride.
An eminent scholar must be assigned the task:
not someone who scribbles little poems,
but a lucid stylist,
a practitioner of unambiguous prose.

The Oriental Gallery

Shadrach, Meshach and Abednego –
three pots from the same kiln.
Their Chinese maker must have been pleased
to see them emerge unscathed from the firing.

He was in the position of God.
They were his faithful servants, showing
by their unblemished complexions and perfect poise
how Nebuchadnezzar can be outsmarted.

Forgive me if I prefer the pieces
on other shelves: bottles with cricked
necks, and the jar that dribbles
its glaze like a sloppily fed baby.

Even more moving are the broken patterns
of pots that wanted to be earth again.

History and Parody

Here we are, for instance, the two of us
on one of those endless walks we used to indulge in,
talking, arguing, sorting out our problems.
The itinerary is pretty much as it was –
the street outside your apartment, the park
with its statues of ridiculous athletes and nudists,
the Old Town and the stretch along the river bank –
though some things may be confusingly transposed.
An impossible silvery-grey light prevails,
but that is all right, as is the sense
of gravity's being skittishly different,
a bit like the mood of one of Goya's engravings.
What do we talk about? Life, love and so on.
You turn to me, using your old gestures,
and I am happy to listen, even while I know
that words are futile and that we are about to be

                                                separated.
In the park, the trees surround us like giant fans.
The paths meet at a fountain which has stopped

                                                burbling.
It is like being on stage, where the third dimension
is in short supply, but at least we are safe from

                                                interlopers.
How ironical now to be wasting our breath on the future!
I smile wryly, but when you ask me what I am smiling

                                                at,
I find I do not have the power to explain
a feeling so selfish and anachronistic.
There are the statues with their muscles and dimples.
They look so real, how can I persuade you
that none of this is happening or needs to be believed?

An Angel

An angel flew by
and the electricity dimmed.
It was like a soft jolt
to the whole of being.
I raised my eyes from the poems
that lay on the kitchen table,
the work of a friend, now dead.

It should not have mattered.
As the light glowed again,
I ought to have continued reading,
but that single pause
terrified me.
We say of the old
that they tremble on the brink.
I found that I was trembling.

Perhaps the black country nights
encourage superstition.
I remembered the angels
that had visited people I knew,
not hurrying past them
and merely stirring the air,
but descending with the all-inclusive
wingspan of annunciation
to obliterate them totally –
and I rose to my feet.

That one brief indecision
of the electric light
in a night of solitude
showed me how weak I was.
The poems on the table
lay where I had left them,
not knowing they had been abandoned.

Realism

I have an idea for a film.
It will begin with a birth;
not the conventional euphemisms,
but pictures of the real thing –
mucky and time-consuming
like some operation in *charcuterie*,
where the child is produced
with a great deal of awkward business
in its ugliest guise:
a little howling blood sausage.

At the end of the film
there will be a death
and this, too, will be shown
in every possible detail:
nothing omitted
from the final grotesque drama
of spasms and incontinence –
just the events as they occur.

And what, you may ask,
will happen in between?
I haven't decided yet,
but at least I can promise
years and years of realism –
what our people have always
      required,
but never yet been given.

Tin Lily

A salvo of blurred words
from the oracular tin lily
on top of the olive-green van.

Just one of those anomalous things
that city-dwellers are no longer surprised by
at certain seasons of the year.

I mean – not the seasons of nature,
but those speedier human phases
that run athwart them.

It was often tricky
to separate the words from the razzmatazz,
and the sentiments could be difficult.

But the way the driver kept his van moving
at a regular walking pace –
anyone could admire that.

Only in eyes here and there
I might see something like resentment,
or terror, or disdain.

Picture an olive-green van
and its four-ways-facing lily
strafing the boulevards.

This is not surrealism,
but an image of the new reality,
a counterblast to Copernicus.

Io

Knots in pinewood,
Argus's peacock-eyes
reproach me daily.

I have learned two things:
that nothing is more implacable
than a betrayed wife's vindictiveness;
that the word for gadfly
has an inner meaning.

Eyebrows Almost Spoke

Eyebrows almost spoke
and I smiled uneasily.

A tongue-tip peered from its mouth
and I wondered why.

A chin shrugged
and I knew that something was going to happen.

An Adam's apple nodded
and I meant to remonstrate.

Shoulders were deep in thought
and I feared the worst.

A back dismissed me
and I went.

On the Subject of Fingers and Thumbs

A blister like a moonstone,
a semi-precious thing –
when as a child I first grew one
I wanted it never to disappear.

It came from digging with a small fork
in my patch of the garden,
from which eventually I collected
a bowl of fat mouse-tailed radishes.

Then the black dirt that packed
hard under my nails,
adding a strange load to my fingers,
gave me a powerful thrill.

I was too young to know why,
but a thought occurred to me:
of saving it all up in a box
for some vague future purpose.

Who knows, I might have acquired enough
to start a new garden.
But the dirt was washed away
and the blister subsided pathetically.

In some ways I am still as childish.
There is a book I love
less for the words it contains
than for the smudge of my thumb on its fore-edge.

The South

The insects formed an *a cappella* choir
and praised God for his almighty heat.
Their song hung like a backcloth,
a seamless silvery-tremulous weaving of sound.
We staggered about like new angels, amazed
at the dazzle and torpor of Paradise.

Lizards paddled on the walls of the house.
Some of the birds could speak a word or two
in our language. A black caterpillar
on its curtain-fringe of little red legs
crossed my path by means of a repeated self-strumming –
a charmed creature, not to be crushed underfoot.

Fed by a system of hidden streams,
there was a rock pool, emerald-green
by daylight, malachite at dusk.
We dipped into this chill element
as if it were possible to taste a little
of whatever spiritual existence we cared to try.

I hesitate to say that I was too lucky,
but what is one to make of experiences
that felt like memory even as they happened?
There were mosquitoes, but their gloating hover
never touched me, and night-lightning
fluttered harmlessly at the horizon.

What the Uneducated Old Woman Told Me

That she was glad to sit down.
That her legs hurt in spite of the medicine.
That times were bad.
That her husband had died nearly thirty years before.
That the war had changed things.
That the new priest looked like a schoolboy and you
        could barely hear him in church.
That pigs were better company, generally speaking, than
          goats.

That no one could fool her.
That both her sons had married stupid women.
That her son-in-law drove a truck.
That he had once delivered something to the President's
          palace.
That his flat was on the seventh floor and that it made
         her dizzy to think of it.
That he brought her presents from the black market.
That an alarm clock was of no use to her.
That she could no longer walk to town and back.
That all her friends were dead.
That I should be careful about mushrooms.
That ghosts never came to a house where a sprig of
        rosemary had been hung.
That the cinema was a ridiculous invention.
That the modern dances were no good.
That her husband had had a beautiful singing voice,
        until drink ruined it.

That the war had changed things.
That she had seen on a map where the war had been
         fought.

That Hitler was definitely in Hell right now.
That children were cheekier than ever.

That it was going to be a cold winter, you could tell
                              from the height of the birds' nests.
That even salt was expensive these days.
That she had had a long life and was not afraid of dying.
That times were very bad.

Apollinaire

As gratuitous as flowers
in the iconography of children,
bombs exploded
on the blank sheet of his mind.

When you gave me his poems,
the strangely fragrant French edition,
I was terrified
by such *boutades* of innocence.

An animating principle
that was not the same as morality
declared itself as I read those pages
full of love and war.

As if the God of the old superstitions
had taken a holiday
under an assumed name,
wearing a jaunty bow-tie.

Picasso drew him
in the form of a coffeepot,
but that was just one of his many
ingenious metamorphoses.

His exotic name suggests
that he was related to Apollo –
or Apollo himself, condemned
to drudge for a while in France.

Surely that would account
for the supererogatory Golden Age
of artistic abundance
when the whole of Paris turned Cubist.

Under his divine inspiration
poems became pictures
of hearts, stars, guns –
everything that they should not be.

I still have your book:
it stays mainly on its shelf,
but I pick it up from time to time
when I want to give myself a fright.

A Box

Imagine a box, not a very big one,
but containing the following indispensable items:
a bed, a soup bowl, a landscape of mists and birches,
the words spoken by a pensive mother,
the absence of a father, several books including
a dictionary with a torn spine
and the works of the troubadours, a small photograph
in which the wince of a girl in sunlight is the main
                                                    point,

a document with a stamp and a signature,
a message received from the friend of a friend,
a journey by train, an odd-looking parcel,
some jokes, anxiety and a final revelation.
Imagine this box, which should not be too large,
then take it and hide it with as little fuss as you can
somewhere you know its contents will be safe.

Piano Variations

The dapper child Mozart
was never invited to our capital.
His contemporary, Carl Ditters von Dittersdorf,
played his violin here, but was overshadowed
by an elephant brought all the way from Samarkand
and remembered even now in the title of one of our folk
dances.

*

Nobody here touches the piano,
but we can boast at least one accordion-player.
And what an amazing invention –
a whole orchestra the size of a small child,
lungs labouring for all to see
as if asthma had been given pitch and harmonic
expressiveness.

*

While squirrels strum the birches
and the spider in the rosebush
crosses her web with a harpist's opportunistic flourish,
the bonnet of our poulterer's truck
is propped open like the lid of a grand piano
from which music will never again be heard.

*

Somebody hoicked up the lid of the concert piano,
the massive black slab,
and at once I thought of resurrection:
the stone at the mouth of the sepulchre
removed, or Jonah's whale
yawning to vomit him out.

The Sea

The tongue tells riddles:
it is as slippery as a fish.
The mind muddles things:
it is as deep as the sea.

We did not go often to the sea. Our few journeys
to the coastal towns were an awkward business.
Where the sea itself was concerned, we were divided.
I was stirred by it to a vague romantic ecstasy, while
                                you
found it an ideal pretext for your bitter Lichtenbergian
                               jokes.
So when I admired the gusto of the fishing smacks,
the gulls' volplaning and the little waves that came
tilting over themselves like ostrich feathers,
you expressed your horror at what you called
'that vast untidiness – like being told someone else's
                               dreams,
or shown a rough draft of the world's most boring epic'.
Our walks on the beach were always perfunctory,
                              ending
with drinks in a café and talk about town.
I think of those outings now, and one occasion in
                            particular,
when I went looking for shells that you described
as 'schoolgirls' knick-knacks . . . maritime *bondieuserie*'.
Later I caught you stooping too, and you explained
that you were trying to find 'the most imperfect pebble –
a very different matter'. I laughed and seized your hand.
There were many questions over which we were at
                              odds,
but none so large or complex or important as the sea.

In a Café

The apple opened
and its perfect flesh disclosed,
you read at once
the brown blush of putrescence.

Can you explain
what all these faces mean?
The different ways
of keeping a skull hidden.

Honour the god
of bluebottles and migraines
with monuments of smoke,
and ash, the turds of cigarettes.

Traditional Stories

Shall I tell you the story about the ladybird
who wanted some new spots?
The old ones were working perfectly well,
but the ladybird decided they looked dowdy
and so she went to see the woman who makes
the pupils for children's eyes –

No? Not that one?

Then would you like to hear the story about the horse
who stands on top of the highest mountain?
On cold mornings the horse breathes heavily
and out of his nostrils come all the clouds
that fill the sky. But the ninety-nine jackdaws
who steal gold rings for the sun –

No? Not that one either?

Then shall I try to remember the story about the snail
who set out on a journey to the centre of his shell?
You know that snails move very slowly,
and this one had been travelling for a whole year
when he met a Gipsy with a magic cooking-pot.
The Gipsy said –

No? Are you quite sure? That's a shame.

Because the only other story I have is the one about the
country girl
who went to live in the big city,
and you've heard that so many times before.

36

Little Man

From behind a plain desk
in the rationed light
of a cubbyhole room
in a clerical building
overlooking a drab back-street,
he asked me a question.
I did not reply at once,
for I had only just noticed
how his silhouette,
head and shoulders,
was eerily imitated
by the knot and swell
of the unpatterned tie
that he wore at his throat.

The People among whom I Live

I admire the people among whom I live,
even though they shoot and bring to the table
the courageous little bird whose cry I have learned to
                                                    interpret
as 'Leave me alone' – repeated again and again
and each syllable released separately
like bubble-capsules from the mouth of a fish.

Even more callous is the way they treat their pigs,
feeding them, pampering them as if they were members
                                                    of the family
to whom they have given the rather grandiose names
of opera singers and *ancien régime* war heroes,
until one morning you see them prodding their rumps
into the bleak interiors of army-style vans.

But there is nothing false about such behaviour.
This is the way they have always conducted their lives,
ever since their ancestors in the muggy glens
first trapped a wild cat by the elaborate ruse
of a delicious buck in a deep hole,
or bribed a falcon to fetch them a hare.

In every other respect, they are straightforward people
and have treated me with nothing but kindness.
Surely their sins are venial?
They do not skulk in passages waiting for the cage
that carries its victim to a third-floor rendezvous,
nor do they drool over a human heart.

Screens

Memory supplies
the illusion that one has lived.
The past is as flat as the rectangle
on which the spectres of film actors,
transmitted there on the backs of dust-motes
across darkened halls,
play their colossal dramas
again and again.

Do you sometimes find it hard
to believe what you are shown:
hero and heroine
wafted through a reverie
of harvests, committee meetings, battlefields,
to arrive at last in each other's arms
while the Orchestra of Destiny
romps triumphantly about them?

I do. And yet once a month
a few of us climb into the schoolmaster's car
and drive to town
to sample the latest offering.
It can be a relief to sit there
and let other people's mind-pictures
cancel my own
with their peremptory flatness.

For the private efforts of memory
are even more bewildering.
How can one justify the mad system
whereby one is oneself the producer
and main protagonist of a work,
the screen on which it falls in ghostly light,
its only audience
and the very dark by which it is surrounded?

Sitting here now, I can identify
a man and a woman
in a small room,
and they are talking intimately.
At the same time I am perfectly aware
that the vision must fade
and my lack of a past be reaffirmed
by a great baulking blankness.

Heaven and Earth

Drizzle-winged, rainbow-flaunting
harbinger of fertility,
the crop-spraying monoplane
swoops on the wheatfields.

It turns and returns
with a diligence and grace
that would inflame the soul
of any earthbound poet.

Heavenly visitations!
I remember how in the city
the entire side of an office block
would glow gold at sunset.

And I would respond like Semele
ravished by her lover,
or the Virgin intruded upon
in her narrow room.

Meditational Exercise

I stood at my window,
thinking about you.
Outdoors, there was the usual business
of a summer's day:
broad sun, the parade
of cumuli in Heaven
and perfect peace –
when, suddenly materializing
miles away,
a helicopter caught my attention.
A moment later
I could see the pilot,
a mere speck of animation
in his snooping glass bubble.

What, I wondered,
did he hope to find
in this part of the country?
My next-door neighbour
stumbling about his flowerbeds
alone as ever –
was he the object of interest?
An old, slow-moving
man of the foothills,
no doubt he would be there
until long after dusk,
wading up to his thighs
in the violet smoulder of cultivated blooms.

This was how he would spend
every day of the season,
preoccupied
with his great labour of love,
tending tight-globed
peony buds,
marigold medallions,
lockets of bleeding heart.
And I would be his sole observer,
caught up in my own
greedy rapture,
the illicit passion of the voyeur.

I did not want the helicopter
to see him too;
I willed it to stay away.
For a few nasty
vertiginous moments
it appeared to be dipping
in our direction,
but the scare passed.
I heard the threatening engine,
and then it swerved off again
almost coquettishly
back into the silence of the clouds.

And what clouds they were!
Incredible structures,
flat-bottomed, but above
as elaborate as palaces,
they moved with the gravity of swans,
each one a separate
world-skimming Laputa
enticing me
on journeys of fabulous speculation.
And if the first to come by
was not quite to my liking,
there were always a hundred others
following in its wake.

Then I noticed
that my neighbour had gone indoors,
leaving his fork
rooted by the tines
and topped-off with a sweat-stained straw hat,
to guard his handiwork.
The helicopter
did not bother to return,
the clouds continued
at their stately pace
and I remained at my window,
thinking about you.

Lines from a Tragedy

Pale twin,
aren't you ashamed
of what we have come to?
Abject crawlers,
porters of heavy flesh,
the unpretty caryatids
of a decaying house . . .

Surely you remember
the great days of our infancy?
Bewhiskered sister,
we did not always wear
such slabs on our toes,
such smoked-looking calluses;
our veins did not always
bulge like this.

Years ago,
before the fall into walking,
we knew how to play
and to touch the world
with our nakedness.
We were as tentative, then,
and as sensitive
as hands.

Like a Mirror

To have possessed you
like a mirror
in which you glanced once,
pulled a face and passed on.

But wait: can mirrors
be said to have memories?
Yes, there is always behind the surface
an inordinate heaviness.

So these touches of tarnish
are an attempt to express
a little of what it remembers.
How sad!

I Disagreed

We visited the famous abbey,
its nettle-sprung ruins.
There was not much to see:
gappy crumble,
bare shelter
for the ghosts of clerics.

Here goose quills
had once illuminated
with their devout scratching
bibles as fat as suitcases.
How unhappy you looked!
'Dead, dead,' you said.

I disagreed.
Looking at the neatly arranged
fragments of saints and angels –
here the peep of a foot,
there the tuck of a girdle –
I thought we might have been standing backstage
with all the props
and that anything was likely to happen.